SCENE BY SCENE
COMPARATIVE WORKBOOK HL17

The Ocean at the End of the Lane

by Neil Gaiman

Theme/Issue - Relationships

Literary Genre

General Vision and Viewpoint

Copyright © 2016 by Amy Farrell.

All rights reserved. No part of this publication may be reproduced, distributed or transmitted in any form or by any means, including photocopying, recording, or other electronic or mechanical methods, without the prior written permission of the publisher, except in the case of brief quotations embodied in critical reviews and certain other noncommercial uses permitted by copyright law. For permission requests, write to the publisher, addressed "Attention: Permissions Coordinator," at the address below.

Scene by Scene
11 Millfield, Enniskerry
Wicklow, Ireland.
www.scenebysceneguides.com

info@scenebysceneguides.com

The Ocean at the End of the Lane Comparative Workbook HL17 by Amy Farrell. —1st ed.
ISBN 978-1-910949-47-4

The Ocean at the End of the Lane Comparative Study Workbook

This workbook is designed to help Leaving Certificate English students become familiar with the Comparative Study modes and to understand how each mode may be applied to *The Ocean at the End of the Lane*.

The Comparative Study Modes at Higher Level for 2017 are:

Theme/Issue

The theme covered in this workbook is Relationships. This theme can be applied to any relationship in a text and covers love, marriage, friendship and family bonds.

Consider the complexities of relationships and the impact they have on characters' lives.

Literary Genre

This mode refers to the way the story is told.

Consider aspects of narration such as the manner and style of narration, characterisation, setting, tension, literary techniques, etc.

The General Vision and Viewpoint

This mode refers to the author's outlook or view of life and how this viewpoint is represented in the text.

Consider whether the text is bright or dark, optimistic or pessimistic, uplifting or bleak, etc.

How Does it Work?

This workbook has three parts, one each for Theme/Issue (our chosen theme for study is Relationships), Literary Genre and General Vision and Viewpoint. Each part has three sections: Know the Text, Know the Mode and Compare the Texts.

Know The Text

These questions are on *The Ocean at the End of the Lane* text and refer specifically to this novel. Through answering these questions you will get to know the text well, while also getting a feel for the Comparative Study mode the questions relate to.

Know the Mode

These questions use 'mode' specific terms and phrases and are intended to help prepare you for tackling exam questions. They focus on the mode itself, rather than the text you have studied. You apply your knowledge of the text to the mode in question.

Compare the Texts

These questions ask you to compare your texts under specific aspects of each mode. It is important that you get used to the idea of comparing and contrasting your chosen texts, as this is what the Comparative Study is all about. It is good practice to think about your texts in terms of their similarities and differences within each mode.

This approach is designed to prevent 'drift' between modes and focuses on analysis and personal response, rather than summary.

KNOW THE TEXT

Theme/Issue - Know the Text

1 What are your first impressions of the boy's relationship with his family?

2 Is he close to his sister? Explain your view.

THE OCEAN AT THE END OF THE LANE – THEME/ISSUE – RELATIONSHIPS

3 In the opening chapters does the boy's father sound like a **fun** father?

4 Does the boy **admire** and **respect** his father?

KNOW THE TEXT

5 What stops the boy from telling his parents the truth about Ursula Monkton? Does this tell you anything about their relationship?

6 The boy doesn't go to his parents when he discovers the hole in his foot. Does this tell you anything about their relationship?

THE OCEAN AT THE END OF THE LANE - THEME/ISSUE - RELATIONSHIPS

7 Does the boy seem isolated from his family to you? Explain your view.

8 What does the bathtub incident reveal to you about the boy's relationship with his father?

KNOW THE TEXT

9 Is the boy brave or foolish to stand up to his father in the fairy circle?

10 "My father did not mention the events of those nights, not then, not later." - Chapter XV.
What does this tell you about their relationship?

THE OCEAN AT THE END OF THE LANE - THEME/ISSUE - RELATIONSHIPS

11 "If I took anything from him...it was the resolve... not to shout at children." - Chapter XV.
What does this tell you about the boy's relationship with his father?

12 "I finally made friends with my father when I entered my twenties...I had been a disappointment to him." - Chapter XV
Do you think the speaker is right here? Did he disappoint his father?

13 Do the boy and his father **communicate**, interact and understand one another well?

14 Does the boy **love** his father?
Use examples to support your view.

THE OCEAN AT THE END OF THE LANE - THEME/ISSUE - RELATIONSHIPS

15 Does the boy **fear** his father?
Use examples to support your view.

16 Does the boy's father **love** his son?
Use examples to support your view.

KNOW THE TEXT

17 What causes problems in this relationship?

18 Is this a positive or negative relationship?

THE OCEAN AT THE END OF THE LANE - THEME/ISSUE - RELATIONSHIPS

19 How does their relationship **change** and **develop**?

20 Is it significant that his father's funeral frames the speaker's visit to the Hempstock farm and his memories of the past?

KNOW THE TEXT

21 Describe the boy's friendship with Lettie.

22 Is this a positive or negative relationship?

THE OCEAN AT THE END OF THE LANE - THEME/ISSUE - RELATIONSHIPS

23 What makes the boy trust Lettie so much?
Is this a powerful friendship?

24 Lettie sacrifices her life for the boy.
What does this tell you about friendship?

KNOW THE MODE

Theme/Issue - Know the Mode

25 Are relationships in this text generally **positive** (warm, supportive, nurturing, genuine) or **negative** (cold, cruel, destructive, false)?

26
What makes relationships in this text complicated and **difficult**?

KNOW THE MODE

27 What would **improve** relationships in this text?

28 How do relationships **change** during the story?

KNOW THE MODE

29 What did **you learn** about relationships from reading this novel?

30 Are relationships **portrayed realistically** in this text? Make use of examples to support the points you make.

31 Are relationships in this story **interesting** and **involving**?

THE OCEAN AT THE END OF THE LANE - THEME/ISSUE - RELATIONSHIPS

32 Did anything about the theme of relationships in this text **shock, upset** or **unsettle** you?

KNOW THE MODE

33 What is the **most signficant relationship** in this text?
What makes it so significant and important?

34 Do relationships in this story bring characters **happiness** or **sorrow**?

KNOW THE MODE

35 Choose **key moments** from this story that highlight relationships in the text.

Theme/Issue - Compare the Texts

36 Were relationships in *The Ocean at the End of the Lane* more positive and supportive than the relationships in your other texts?
Give specific examples.

37 Rank the relationships you have studied in your various texts from most positive to most negative. Add a note to explain your choices.

38 Were relationships in *The Ocean at the End of the Lane* the most engaging and interesting that you have studied? Explain your choice.

39 Rank the relationships you have studied in your various texts from most interesting to least interesting. Add a note to explain your choices.

40 Did you **learn most** about the theme of relationships from this text or another text on your comparative course?

41 What **similarities** do you notice in the theme of relationships in this text and your other comparative texts?

COMPARE THE TEXTS

THE OCEAN AT THE END OF THE LANE - THEME/ISSUE - RELATIONSHIPS

42 What **differences** do you notice in the theme of relationships in this text and your other comparative texts?

COMPARE THE TEXTS

Literary Genre - Know the Text

43 How is this story told? (Consider the novel format)

44 Why is the story told in this way?
What is the effect of this?

45 What was your initial view of the boy?

46 How does Gaiman develop the boy's character?

THE OCEAN AT THE END OF THE LANE - LITERARY GENRE

47 What details show that the speaker was an unhappy child? How is this picture created?

48 Does the boy's age add anything to the story?

49 How does Neil Gaiman present Ursula Monkton as an **evil**, threatening **character**?
Consider her appearance, her actions and the things she says.

50 "the thing that floated above me was huge and greedy, and it wanted to take me to the attic, and when it tired of me it would make my daddy kill me." - Chapter VIII.
Is this a horror story?

51 How does Neil Gaiman build **tension** and **suspense** throughout the episode with Ursula Monkton?

52 What does the Ursula Monkton episode reveal to you about the boy's character?

KNOW THE TEXT

53 How do **descriptions** of the Ursula Monkton creature and the cleaners add to the story?

54 The author ratchets up the tension with one exhilarating, frightening event after another. Outline the chain of tense events. Which one did you find most frightening/ tense?

| 55 | The story is told by the boy's older self. Does this add anything to the story? Does it take anything from the story? |

| 56 | "I ran towards the darkness." - Chapter XIV How does the boy's decision to sacrifice himself to the hunger birds add to the story? How does it add to his character? |

KNOW THE TEXT

57 How important is **memory** in this story?

58 Do you find the speaker's revised memory at the end frustrating? Is it necessary for the story?

59 Consider Gaiman's use of **symbols** in this story. Does the Hempstock farm symbolise something? What do the Hempstock women represent to the speaker?

Literary Genre - Know the Mode

60 Did **you** enjoy the **storyline** of the text?
Was it exciting/compelling/tense/emotional?
Why/why not?

61 Is there just one **plot** or many plots?
What connections can you make between the storylines?

62 What three things interested **you** most in the story?

63 Are **characters** vivid, realistic and well-developed?

64 Do **you** empathise or **identify** with any character(s)?
Did you become involved in this story or care about the characters? Use examples.

65 Who was your **favourite character**? What aspects of this character did you enjoy?

66 Consider the boy as the novel's **hero**. What made the boy a **memorable** or **interesting** character?

67 Who was your **least favourite character**? What aspects of this character did you dislike? What made them a memorable or interesting character?

KNOW THE MODE

68 Is the story humorous or tragic, romantic or realistic? Explain using examples.

69 To what **genre** does it belong?
What aspects of this genre did **you** enjoy?
Is it Romance, Thriller, Horror, Action/Adventure, Historical, Fantasy, Science-fiction, Satire, etc.?

70 How does the author create **suspense**, **high emotion** and **excitement** in the text? What **techniques** does he use to good advantage?

KNOW THE MODE

71 Consider the author's use of **tension** and **resolution** in the novel. What are the major **tensions/problems/conflicts** in the text? Are they **resolved** or not?

THE OCEAN AT THE END OF THE LANE - LITERARY GENRE

72 Did the author make use of any striking patterns of **imagery** or **symbols** to add to the story?

73 How does the author make use of the **unexpected** in this text? What did this add to the story? (Think about key moments here.)

KNOW THE MODE

74 What is the **climax** (high point) of the story?

75 What did **you** think of this moment?
How did it make **you feel**?

76 Comment on the **language** of the novel. How does dialogue and description add to the story?

77 Comment on the **pacing** of the novel. How does this add to the story?

KNOW THE MODE

78 Comment on the **setting** of the novel.
Consider time, place, and specific locations such as the boy's home and the Hempstock farm. How does setting add to your understanding of the characters and their story?

THE OCEAN AT THE END OF THE LANE - LITERARY GENRE

79 Was anything about this novel **moving** or **emotional**?
Think of moments in the novel that you responded to. What made them moving? How did this add to the story?

80 On a scale of one to ten, how much did you enjoy the **ending**? What was satisfying/unsatisfying about it? Was anything left unanswered?

81 The experiences of seeing a play, reading a novel and viewing a film are very different.
What aspects of the **novel form** worked well in this story, in your opinion?

82 What did **you** like about **the way** the story was told?
*Mention aspects of storytelling and literary techniques that **you** found enjoyable. Refer to key moments.*

83 Identify **key moments** in the novel that illustrate Literary Genre (the way the story is told). Clearly **define literary techniques/aspects of narrative** in your analysis.

Literary Genre - Compare the Texts

84 Did **you** like the way this story was told more than your other comparative texts?
State what you enjoyed most about each.

85 Is *The Ocean at the End of the Lane* more **exciting** than your other texts?
Consider tension, pacing, suspense, conflict and the unexpected.

86

Are characters more engaging in this novel than in your other texts?
Refer to each of your texts in you answer.

87
Is the **setting** more effective in telling this story than in your other texts?
Refer to each of your texts in your answer.

88 Is this story more **unpredictable** than your other texts?
Refer to each of your texts in your answer.

89 Did this novel have greater **emotional power** than your other texts?
Was emotional power created in a more interesting way here or in a different text?

90 What **similarities** do you notice in the Literary Genre of this novel and your other comparative texts?
Mention specific aspects of narrative.

COMPARE THE TEXTS

91 What **differences** do you notice in the Literary Genre of this novel and your other comparative texts?
Mention specific aspects of narrative.

COMPARE THE TEXTS

General Vision and Viewpoint - Know the Text

92 How does nobody attending the boy's birthday and his kitten dying, contribute to the mood of the opening section?

93 How does the discovery of the dead man and the manner of his death affect the mood of the story?

| 94 | How does the speaker's dream where he is held down and wakes up choking, contribute to the atmosphere? |

| 95 | Is the boy lonely and isolated? Does this suggest anything about life? |

THE OCEAN AT THE END OF THE LANE - GENERAL VISION AND VIEWPOINT

96 Consider the scene as the boy tries to escape Ursula and reach the Hempstock farm. Is his a difficult struggle? Does this tell us anything about Gaiman's outlook?

97 "There was nothing to scare me but shadows..."
- Chapter XII
Does Neil Gaiman depict the world as a frightening, threatening or magical place?

KNOW THE TEXT

98 "Nobody cares...come to us. One step is all it will take." - Chapter XII
Does the author present the world as a cruel, uncaring place?

99 What does the boy's devotion to Lettie suggest about life?

THE OCEAN AT THE END OF THE LANE - GENERAL VISION AND VIEWPOINT

100 What do the boy's and Lettie's acts of sacrifice suggest about goodness, strength and bravery?

101 What does the boy's experience in Lettie's Ocean suggest about life and our world?

102 Is there a **sadness** to this story?

103 'You don't pass or fail at being a person, dear.'
What point is the author making about life, through Ginnie Hempstock?
Is the speaker sure of his place in the world?

THE OCEAN AT THE END OF THE LANE - GENERAL VISION AND VIEWPOINT

104 Is it difficult to be a child and cope with the world in Gaiman's view?
Is life complicated and confusing?
Is this what this story is about?

105 How does the frightening, gruesome **imagery** contribute to the General Vision and Viewpoint? What does it tell us about the author's view of life?

KNOW THE TEXT

106 How does the closing section make you feel?
Is this a happy ending?
Use 'I' statements to develop your Personal Response.

107 What is Neil Gaiman telling us about life in this story?
What is Neil Gaiman's message?
Is his outlook positive or negative, in your view?

General Vision and Viewpoint - Know the Mode

108 Identify bright/hopeful/optimistic aspects of the novel.

109 Identify dark/hopeless/pessimistic aspects of the novel.

THE OCEAN AT THE END OF THE LANE – GENERAL VISION AND VIEWPOINT

110 Is this text **optimistic** or **pessimistic**? Explain. *Consider characters' happiness, imagery, atmosphere, future prospects, etc.*

111 On a scale of one to ten, how optimistic is this text?

112

Identify the **aspects of life** that the author concentrates on.
Are they positive or negative?
Consider loneliness, fear, isolation, bravery, determination, love, etc.

113 What **comments** do characters make on their **society** and the problems they're facing?

KNOW THE MODE

114 Are characters happy or unhappy?

115 What makes characters in this story happy and fulfilled?

116 What makes characters in this story unhappy and unfulfilled?

117 Are **relationships** destructive or nurturing? What do they reveal about life, as we see characters supported/thwarted in their efforts to grow/mature?

118 Are **imagery** and **language** bright or dark in the text? (Tone of the text)

119 What is the **mood** of this text?

120 What does this story **teach us about life?**
What do we learn about life's hardships? Are struggles overcome? Is determination rewarded? Is life difficult or joyful?

121 How do you **feel** as you read this novel?
Refer to key moments to anchor your answer.

122 How do you **feel** at the **end**?

| 123 | Are **questions** raised by the text **resolved** by the end?
Are they resolved **happily** or **unhappily**? |
|---|---|

124 Are **you hopeful** or **despairing** regarding the prospects for human **happiness** in this story?
Are characters likely to be happy?

125 Identify the **key moments** in the novel that illustrate the General Vision and Viewpoint of the text.

General Vision and Viewpoint - Compare the Texts

126 Is life happier for characters in this story than in your other comparative texts? Explain.

COMPARE THE TEXTS

127 Do characters in this text face more obstacles and difficulties than in your other texts?
Who struggles most?

128 Are characters in this text **rewarded more** for their struggles than in your other texts?
By overcoming adversity, do they achieve true happiness and contentment in a way that is not realised in your other texts?

129
Is this the brightest, most hopeful and triumphant text you have studied? Explain why its message is more or less positive than your other texts.

130

Which of your chosen texts was the bleakest and most upsetting or depressing?

Explain why it was more negative than your other texts. What made them more positive?

COMPARE THE TEXTS

131 Plot your three texts on a scale of one to ten, from darkest (most pessimistic) to brightest (most optimistic). Add points to explain their position.

THE OCEAN AT THE END OF THE LANE – GENERAL VISION AND VIEWPOINT

132 What **similarities** do you notice in the General Vision and Viewpoint of this text and your other comparative texts?

COMPARE THE TEXTS

133 What **differences** do you notice in the General Vision and Viewpoint of this text and your other comparative texts?

COMPARE THE TEXTS

www.ingramcontent.com/pod-product-compliance
Lightning Source LLC
Chambersburg PA
CBHW050714090526
44587CB00019B/3375